50 ROMAN FINDS FROM THE PORTABLE ANTIQUITIES SCHEME

John Pearce and Sally Worrell

AMBERLEY

First published 2020

Amberley Publishing
The Hill, Stroud
Gloucestershire, GL5 4EP

www.amberley-books.com

Copyright © John Pearce and Sally Worrell, 2020

The right of John Pearce and Sally Worrell to be
identified as the Authors of this work has been
asserted in accordance with the Copyrights, Designs
and Patents Act 1988.

ISBN 978 1 4456 8684 4 (print)
ISBN 978 1 4456 8685 1 (ebook)

British Library Cataloguing in Publication Data.
A catalogue record for this book is available from
the British Library.

Origination by Amberley Publishing.
Printed in the UK.

Contents

Acknowledgements

This book publishes a selection of fifty Roman finds from England and Wales documented by the Portable Antiquities Scheme (PAS) up to June 2019. Sally Worrell has worked for twenty years for the PAS, first as Finds Liaison Officer for Hampshire and since 2003 as National Finds Advisor for later prehistory and the Roman period. John Pearce teaches Roman archaeology at King's College London. We are currently responsible for writing the annual report for the journal *Britannia* on Roman objects documented by the PAS. The abundance of Roman artefacts makes it near impossible to select only fifty representative finds and our choice inevitably reflects our own biases. We hope that readers will wish to make their own selection among the thousands of Roman objects to be encountered on the Scheme's publicly accessible database: www.finds.org.uk.

 This book could only be written thanks to the work of all staff of the PAS, which was established in 1997 by Roger Bland and directed by him until 2015, when he was succeeded by Michael Lewis. Space does not allow us here to acknowledge by name all the individuals with whom we have worked, but we are especially sorry that David Williams, formerly FLO for Surrey, is no longer with us to run his unforgiving eye over our text. We express our gratitude to Justine Bayley, David Breeze, Hella Eckardt, Michel Feugère, Martin Henig, Ralph Jackson, Sam Moorhead and Will Wootton for their comments on objects which we have published in *Britannia* and elsewhere, and to Caroline Birch for kindly reading and commenting on this entire text in draft. We are indebted too to Martin Millett and Tim Schadla-Hall for the opportunity to work on metal-detected material from East Yorkshire and for their continuing support. For any errors in what follows, the responsibility however is ours alone. John Casey and Jenny Price, both of whom sadly died in recent years (2017 and 2019 respectively), were a source of encouragement and advice on Roman objects and careers from student days onwards.

 For individual objects we give their unique identifier which allows them to be located on the PAS website. If no specific date is given then objects cannot be dated more closely than to the Roman period (*c.* AD 43 – AD 410). In many cases we have reproduced only a single view of an object – many more can be found on the PAS website. Unless otherwise stated, images are used courtesy of the Portable Antiquities Scheme under Creative Commons by Attribution licences (2.0 and 4.0). The distribution maps in chapters 1 and 5 were created respectively by Katie Robbins and Angie Bolton, to whom we extend our thanks. We specifically acknowledge the kind permission to use the following illustrations:

Christie's, helmet, Crosby Garrett (16); Tony Wilmott / Historic England, Birdoswald cemetery excavation (20); Peter Halkon, Apollo figurine, Hayton (25); Somerset County Council and South West Heritage Trust, Capricorn, Burrington (36); Norfolk County Council Environment Service, knife handle, Ditchingham (98); Peter Halkon, wax spatula handle, Hayton (119); Chiz Harward, key, Southwark (131); Peter Halkon, mouse, Hayton (142); Nick Griffiths, strainer bowl, Kingston Deverill (145).

Foreword

The places in which we live and work have a long past, but one that is not always obvious in the landscape around us. This is a forgotten past. Most of us know little about the people who once lived in our communities fifty years ago, let alone 500, or even 5,000 years past. Like us, they lived, played and worked here, in this place, but we know almost nothing of them.

History books tell us about royalty, aristocrats and important churchmen, but most others are forgotten by time. The only evidence for many of these people is the objects that they left behind, sometimes buried on purpose, but more often than not lost by chance. Occasionally, through archaeological fieldwork, we can place these objects in a context that allows us to better understand the past, but nowadays excavation is mostly development led, so only takes place when a new building, road or service pipe is being constructed.

A unique way of understanding the past is through the finds recorded through the Portable Antiquities Scheme, of which those chosen here by Sally Worrell (National Finds Advisor for later prehistory and the Roman period) and John Pearce are just fifty of over 600,000 from the Roman period on its database (www.finds.org.uk). These finds were all discovered by the public, most by metal-detector users, searching in places archaeologists are unlikely to go or otherwise excavate. As such they provide important clues of underlying archaeology that (once recorded) help archaeologists understand our past – a past of the people, found by the people.

Some of these finds are truly magnificent, others less imposing. Yet, like pieces in a jigsaw puzzle they are often meaningless alone, but once placed together paint a picture. These finds therefore allow us to understand the story of people who once lived here, in Roman Britain.

Dr Michael Lewis
Head of Portable Antiquities & Treasure
British Museum

Chapter 1
The Portable Antiquities Scheme and Roman Britain

The Portable Antiquities Scheme is one of the most important innovations in British archaeology in recent decades, documenting hundreds of thousands of objects which would otherwise have been lost from our shared heritage. This book chooses fifty finds of Roman date to illuminate the society and culture of Roman Britain. Some exceptional discoveries are now iconic objects, such as the Crosby Garrett helmet and the Staffordshire Moorlands pan, but most are ordinary artefacts which, nonetheless, offer a pathway into the Roman period. Before we examine individual discoveries, it is important to briefly set the scene, first by describing the Portable Antiquities Scheme (PAS) and second by introducing the Roman province from which these artefacts come.

Many archaeological objects are discovered by members of the public, especially by metal-detector users. Established in 1997 and expanded to cover England and Wales in 2003, the PAS documents these finds, which would otherwise go unrecorded. It comprises Finds Liaison Officers based in different regions of England and Wales, administered by a central unit in the British Museum and supported by specialist advisors. The PAS also facilitates the reporting of discoveries which fall within the terms of the Treasure Act (1996, revised 2002). Since 1997 the discoveries documented by the PAS have become a major new resource for archaeological research, including both the records of the objects themselves and, crucially, their find-spots, without which their value for study of the past is greatly impoverished.

Roman finds are the most numerous of any period, now comprising *c.* 625,000 of the 1.42 million objects recorded by June 2019. Their sheer abundance and diversity compared to other periods is a sign of the fundamental changes in Britain under Roman rule. Before the campaigns of Julius Caesar, Britain lay on the edge of Roman consciousness, an island in the vast ocean, home to painted barbarians, as the Romans thought. Drawn increasingly into Roman political and economic systems after Caesar's invasions (55 and 54 BC), the formal establishment of the province did not begin for another century. From the invasion ordered by the emperor Claudius in AD 43, attracted by the gloss a triumph on the world's edge would bring to his new regime, Roman rule lasted until the early fifth century AD. It ended with secession and rebellion, amidst the empire's wider fragmentation. During the half millennium of Roman contact and control the island was transformed, its landscape studded with towns, villas and frontier works, and its resources used on a previously unseen scale. Two processes were responsible for these transformations: Rome's exploitation of its new province and long-term trends beginning in preceding eras, including population growth, technological change, economic intensification and escalating inequality.

Looting by Rome's armies gave way to long-term extraction of tax, metals, men and grain, but Britain did not solely become an imperial society through direct exploitation. It was also integrated into political and economic networks within which people and ideas, materials and things moved and mixed more easily than ever before, from the Atlantic to the Eurasian Steppe. In making Britain part of a wider empire, some Britons became agents of Roman power, such as magistrates and soldiers. Incorporation within an empire also transformed behaviour. The appeal of Rome is well illustrated, for instance by the paraphernalia of wine serving and drinking (strainers, cups and amphorae, for example), or the equipment for writing (styli, inkwells, wax spatulas and so on, as well as surviving documents). The profusion of motifs from Greco-Roman art, deities, genre figures or exotic animals, on objects large and small, imported and made in Britain, shows the changing tastes of artisans and consumers. But not all change was a simple shift towards practices imported from the Mediterranean. Personal appearance – skin, nails, hair and so on – was manipulated using grooming tools which had come into use in the Iron Age, and the common modes of provincial dress had developed before Roman conquest. Many decorative techniques, for example enamelling and 'swirly' styles, also owed their genesis to Iron Age art, though their application extended enormously during the Roman period, partly because of adoption by groups like soldiers.

Objects are crucial to illuminating these changes but they also had an 'active' power of their own, being used by individuals to negotiate their position within provincial society, to show their sophistication and familiarity with Greco-Roman elite culture, for example, or to mark their belonging to a particular group, such as soldiers. Our focus will mainly lie on the insights gained from objects which fall into the artefact category used by Roman archaeologists known as 'small finds'. These comprise objects not included among the typical 'bulk' finds discovered on archaeological sites, such as ceramics, or environmental evidence such as plant or faunal remains. Made in diverse materials, mainly but not exclusively metal (but also bone, ivory, jet, amber), and usually portable, 'small finds' typically require more detailed recording to document their form, purpose and 'biography'. Most can be attributed to quite specific functions – for work, worship, dress and play – and have become central to interpreting the changes which happened following Britain's incorporation in the Roman world. In almost every 'small find' category a major body of new data is now available for study thanks to the PAS; for example, 30,370 brooches of first-century BC to fourth-century AD date have been recorded up to June 2019.

Our objects largely derive from the countryside of Roman Britain as Roman cities and military camps are often legally protected by scheduling as ancient monuments and are not susceptible to metal detecting where they lie within modern built-up areas. Metal detectorists focus on landscapes where the plough brings artefacts within reach of their detectors' sensors, so many more finds come from the intensely farmed arable zones of central, southern and, above all, eastern England than from the uplands of western and northern England and Wales. In some exceptional circumstances the repertoire of materials extends beyond metals, especially on the Thames foreshore in London or among the finds from the Tees at Piercebridge, County Durham, where a garrison guarded the river crossing. Some had been dropped into the water as gifts to gods; others were rubbish washed out of riverbanks. On Cumbria's Irish Sea coast, the human remains and grave goods eroded from graves in the dunes at Beckfoot represent another exceptional discovery. Occasionally objects have been found *in situ* where they had been deliberately placed in the past, especially in graves, coin hoards and so-called 'structured deposits', i.e. artefacts buried together to hide them or to propitiate deities. In some cases, archaeological excavation has been able to document the objects' context and tell a fuller story behind their burial.

In the following chapters we use examples of single objects found during detecting and some assemblages where subsequent excavation has taken place, to explore the encounter between different cultural traditions, Roman and local. We have adapted some of the 'small finds' categories used by Roman archaeologists as a structure, considering symbols and tools of Roman power (Chapter 2), ways of worshipping the gods (Chapter 3), strategies for influencing fortune and fate (Chapter 4), dressing and styling the body (Chapters 5 and 6), artefacts for enabling movement of people, things and information (Chapter 7) and finally objects for making homes (Chapter 8).

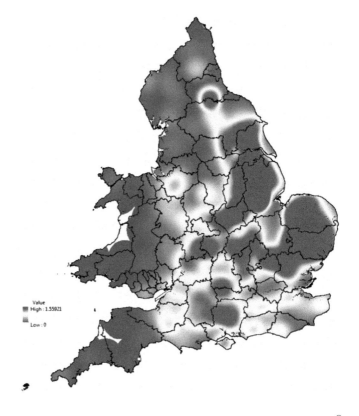

Value
High : 1.55921
Low : 0

Heat map showing the distribution of non-coin objects recorded by the PAS. Red indicates higher find densities, blue lower. (Katie Robbins)

Miniature garnet head of the philosopher Socrates, an emblem of the sophistication aspired to by Romano-British elites, Brampton, Norfolk. (NMS-8B3A40)

Small, copper alloy bound captive, a symbol of the enslavement for some which followed Roman conquest, Andover, Hants. (HAMP-378231)

Foreshore at the Roman fort at Beckfoot, Cumbria, looking towards south-west Scotland. (Photograph by John Pearce)

Excavation of the Kingston Deverill hoard of metal vessels. (WILT-92B052)

Chapter 2
Roman Power in Objects

The conquest of Britain was a piecemeal process, taking decades to bring Roman arms from the south coast to Scotland. A frontier zone in northern Britain was not definitively established until almost a century after the AD 43 invasion under Claudius. 'Conquest' was a product of diplomacy as much as violence and much of Britain saw only a brief large-scale military presence. The lasting garrisons for legionary and auxiliary units were located mainly in northern and western Britain, many of the latter in the north Pennines in association with Hadrian's Wall and the roads leading to it. Some limited reconfiguration in the third and fourth centuries saw new coastal forts and garrisoning of soldiers in some towns.

The experience of Roman authority was therefore diverse. Conquest included a violent grab of land and mineral resources, slave-taking and military levies, as well as tax and tribute. Maintenance of authority was partly enabled by soldiers, the symbolic presence of the emperor and a literate bureaucracy. The tablets from the auxiliary fort at Vindolanda, just south of Hadrian's Wall in Northumberland, illustrate this especially well, with their minute documentation of the garrison's activity. But this was not only a top-down system of oppression. Where soldiers were stationed, communities developed including military dependents and households, as well as native Britons and traders drawn by the economic opportunities offered in supplying the army, or of joining up. And local elites were co-opted into Roman rule, turning Iron Age kings into magistrates of the city states (*civitates*) into which Britannia was divided and to which most provincial government was devolved.

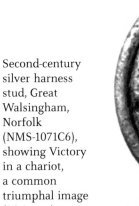

Second-century
silver harness
stud, Great
Walsingham,
Norfolk
(NMS-1071C6),
showing Victory
in a chariot,
a common
triumphal image
(16.4 mm).

Reconstruction of the western fort gate at Arbeia, South Shields, gateway to Hadrian's Wall at the Tyne mouth. (Photograph by John Pearce, by kind permission of Arbeia South Shields Roman Fort and Tyne & Wear Archives & Museums)

13

For inhabitants of the Roman empire the emperor was rarely encountered in person but ubiquitous as a symbol, above all on coins which carried his image and titles. Larger imperial portraits were also created. The biographer of emperors, Suetonius, tells us that statues of Titus (AD 79–81) were widespread in Britain, no doubt made using the province's metals. However, statues of Titus or any other emperor are extraordinarily rare. Usually fragments alone have escaped the recycling which was their typical fate. Only in one case has a more complete portrait been documented by the PAS: the 'Brackley Head', a half-life-sized image, found during ploughing in 1976. Its features closely resemble those of the emperor Marcus Aurelius (AD 161–80), but the stylized cork-screw curls of the thick hair and full beard come from local artistic tradition. The deep blue glass eyes, unusual survivals for typically blank-eyed bronzes, give the head an unusually captivating character. Mounted on a frame, the emperor's head was light enough to be carried in a procession, perhaps in a festival at the rural settlement near the Oxfordshire border where it was found. Pieces of an equestrian statue from North Carlton, which perhaps once graced the forum in Lincoln, hint tantalisingly at the form larger images took.

Bust of Marcus Aurelius, Brackley, 162 mm high. (Photograph by Stuart Laidlaw)

Above: Fragments of a life-size bronze equestrian statue, from the neck and jaw and gilded mane (not to scale), North Carlton, Lincs. (LIN-31B698)

Right: Equestrian statue of Marcus Aurelius, replica in the Piazza del Campidoglio, Rome. (Photograph by John Pearce)

As well as his face, the emperor's authority was also represented by his name, as a Somerset lead 'pig' or ingot shows. The claim by the historian Tacitus that the Roman conquest was motivated by Britain's mineral wealth is borne out by the opening of mines on the Mendip Hills soon after AD 43. The Westbury 'pig' illustrates their continuing exploitation more than a century later. Lead and silver occur in the same ore and lead 'pigs' were therefore produced at *argentaria* (silver mines). Pressed into the moulds in which the 'pigs' were cast was a retrograde text (i.e. written in reverse) which reproduced the owner's name on the ingot's surface. In 30-mm-high letters the inscription advertises this 'pig' as belonging to the co-emperors Marcus Aurelius (AD 161–180) and Lucius Verus (AD 161–69), made as payment in exchange for the mining concession. The epithet *Armeniaci*, 'victors in Armenia', appears alongside the abbreviated imperial names, a title awarded for the capture of Armenia's mountain capital in AD 163. Once news of victory reached the Mendips, the moulds were updated to demonstrate the loyalty of the managers of these strategically important silver mines. The names celebrated imperial triumph and unity as well as deterring theft. However, like many 'pigs' found around the Mendip edges, the Westbury ingot was 'lost in transit' after leaving the lead field. The brutal control of forced labour, used for mines and in other areas of economic activity, is illustrated by occasional finds like the Kingsworthy iron shackle.

Lead pig, Westbury, 52 cm long, 19 kg in weight.

Iron shackle, Kingsworthy, Hants. (HAMP-C45106)

3. Enamelled pan (WMID-3FE965), AD 122–300, Staffordshire Moorlands.

For 300 years after its inception (AD 122), Hadrian's Wall was the most monumental element of a grid of garrisons and roads which formed Britain's frontier. Whatever the Wall's purpose – customs barrier, imperial monument or defensive obstacle – a group of enamel-decorated pans celebrates its existence. These small flat-handled dippers carry inscriptions around the rim naming forts on the wall. Two examples have been documented by the Portable Antiquities Scheme. One, a fragment from Bowers Gifford and North Benfleet, carries part of two forts' names, as well as crenellations representing the wall. Despite the loss of its handle and base, the other, found at Ilam in the Peak District, is the most striking of the group. As well as naming four forts at the western end of Hadrian's wall (Bowness-on-Solway, Drumburgh, Stanwix and Castlesteads), it places them 'on the line of the Wall of Aelius', and names the pan's likely owner as one Draco. Beneath the text swirling polychrome enamel circles substitute for crenellations, a decorative technique originating in northern Europe but favoured by military consumers. To the veterans who took such pans home, the sequence of garrison names recalled a route endlessly marched from the Solway flatlands to the Pennine Hills.

Staffordshire Moorlands Pan, 90 mm diameter. (Photograph by Stuart Laidlaw)

Fragment of a decorated pan, Bowers Gifford and North Benfleet, Essex. (ESS-5945F8)

Silver denarius of Hadrian, AD 119–122, Fleet Marston, Bucks. (BUC-4992D8)

The soldiers who fought in Rome's campaigns and garrisoned the frontier are not easily found among PAS objects. Weapons are not common metal-detected discoveries and most military finds comprise scraps of armour or horse gear. Occasionally, however, more complete objects survive, illuminating both extraordinary and typical equipment. The Crosby Garrett helmet, for use in spectacular military drills, exemplifies the former. Its visor shows an impassive youth, the headpiece a 'Phrygian cap' which marks the wearer as 'Persian' or Eastern. Most such helmets show exotic figures, but this form is not yet paralleled among other surviving helmets. Showing a likely Trojan in some mythological encounter acted out on the parade ground, it would have been a marker of equestrian virtuosity for the grizzled veteran behind the mask. By contrast the Over Kellet shield boss is a component of a more typical weapon but a rare survival, still with its bronze gleam. Both objects are found at a distance from known garrisons, the helmet on a farmstead high on the Cumbrian hills, the shield boss near a river crossing for the Roman road running north from Lancaster. The Dutch archaeologist Johann Nikolay has revealed the complex biographies of militaria like these, found far from their garrison homes through looting, re-use as scrap, or as mementoes of service for ex-soldiers.

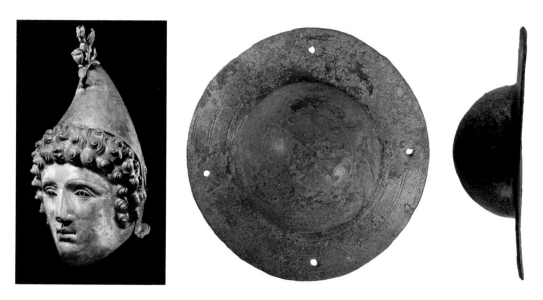

Above left: Crosby Garret helmet, 407 mm high. (© Christie's)

Above right: Shield boss, Over Kellet, Lancs. (LANCUM-D876DE)

Extensive settlements developed around Roman garrisons, housing communities whose origins lay across the Roman world. Epitaphs from the fort of Old Carlisle, found during building repair, illustrate the use by one such community of commemoration in Latin, a habit borrowed from soldiers. The largest fragment lists at least seven individuals, adults and children. One of the dead, Panno... (part of the name is broken off), took his or her name from the provinces of Pannonia (Hungary and adjacent areas). Three individuals share the name Aurelius, suggesting that the epitaph dates to the early third century AD when many provincials took the family name of the emperor Caracalla, following his declaration of universal Roman citizenship. The laconic text gives names and ages at death, typically abbreviated to VA (*vixit annos...*). Words are separated by elegant 'leaf-stops' and the capitals are well cut, though no trace shows of the red paint which once improved their legibility. What survives hints at the labour of memorial making, shaping the stone, chiselling a frame and smoothing a panel to carry writing before setting out and cutting the inscription. The urns filled with cremated bone found in the dunes by the Roman fort at Beckfoot a few miles away or in excavations at Birdoswald on the wall illustrate the likely burial style for Panno... and his family or friends.

Above left: Tombstone from Old Carlisle, 660 mm x 500 mm.

Above right: Greyware jar used as cremation urn, plus cup used as lid, Beckfoot, Cumbria. (LANCUM-413CA5)

Excavation of Roman cremation burials, Birdoswald, 2009. (Photograph by John Pearce, by kind
permission of Historic England)

Like modern empires, Rome depended on manpower from its subject peoples to maintain its armies. Recruitment of auxiliary units included mass levies and individuals electing to sign up. A soldier's salary and the reward of Roman citizenship for veterans gave better prospects than farm life. One such recruit was Velvotigernos, sailor in the Rhine fleet for twenty-six years from AD 124 and awarded citizenship on 19 November 150. His career and privileges are revealed by a bronze diploma, one of three recorded by the PAS, found west of the fort at Lanchester and now displayed in the Museum of Archaeology, Durham University. It gives his father's name, Magiotigernos, and his British origin, though no wife. Assuming Velvotigernos had returned to his family home, his life was framed by the Roman army. As a boy he would have seen the Pennines garrisoned and Hadrian's Wall built. In his own service he would have moved men and materiel along the Rhine and its tributaries as Roman power pushed east into Germany.

As a recruit, his life was measured by the Roman calendar, completing his service in a year named after its consuls and with months adopted from the Roman year. An exceptional fragment from Hambledon derives from a time-measuring device, preserving sub-divisions of the month of August, named after the first emperor. This was a water clock (*clepsydra*) in bowl form, with the calendar set out in peg holes on its rim. It recorded the passing of the hours, which were measured as a proportion of the duration of daylight and so varied in length during the year. Water drained through a hole in the base, progressively dropping below lines incised on the bowl's sides to mark those hours; the distance between those lines varied with the time of year. The Hambledon fragment, one of only three such clocks known, shows how time was re-set to a Roman standard.

Above and left: Diploma – part of sheet 1 (*c.* 55 mm long, 1.5 mm thick) and the name of Velvotigernos.

Below: Water clock fragment, Hambledon, Hants. (SUSS-BA3CBE)

Much more common than arms are elements of military dress. In the third and fourth centuries AD the large belts worn by soldiers became more elaborate, with the buckles, stiffeners and strap ends decorated in a range of techniques; for example, enamelling (like the third-century example from Kingsclere), openwork and 'chip-carving', the latter named after a carpentry technique. An openwork belt buckle from Chepstow, with a frame, tongue and plate still hinged together, dates to the last decades of Roman rule. On the buckle frame two horses' heads meet, framing the buckle's two-pronged tongue. The plate is decorated with a horse, trotting right, with a pelta (semi-circular) motif above it, representing a helmeted rider. On the back are lugs to attach the plate to a leather belt. The closest parallel is a buckle plate from Argeliers, south-western France, of a type known as the 'Pseudo-Hispanic' belt. The presence of such a buckle in south-east Wales, near a strategic river crossing, may reflect the stationing of a soldier recruited from, or previously posted to, Gaul or Hispania.

Above left: Chepstow buckle, 97 mm long.

Above right: Third-century AD belt plate, Kingsclere, Hants. (HAMP1515)

Chapter 3
Worshipping the Gods

Rome introduced a new pantheon of deities to Britain, including gods of Rome herself, gods of Greco-Roman myth, and gods adopted during Rome's political and military expansion. In Britain these new deities, including the pervasive *numen* (divine spirit) of the emperor, mingled with gods of the island's prehistoric past. The latter were made visible by the new habit of naming gods in inscriptions and making images of them. These fundamental changes to worship, including the commissioning of statues of deities, building sanctuaries to house them and offering prayers in Latin, were as significant as the arrival of new gods.

Figurine of Apollo from Hayton, E. Yorks. The maker has misinterpreted the lyre as a support for the god to lean on. (Photograph by Mike Park)

Of images made in stone, clay, wood and metal, the latter are documented in their hundreds by the PAS. A handful of fragments of larger statues are vastly outnumbered by the many figurines, usually *c.* 50–150 mm high in copper alloy, created as offerings to honour the gods and to make the god present to worshippers in household shrines. Images were also created on votive leaves, thin sheets of metal decorated with relief images of the gods. The hoard of metal objects buried in a vessel near Bury St Edmunds includes fragments of copper alloy leaves, as well as items of priests' regalia. These include parts of a chain-linked headdress which would have been attached to a fabric or leather cap, and bird- and spear-shaped tips from staffs of sceptres carried by priests or their attendants.

Iron Age and Roman tradition placed a shared importance on animal sacrifice. In the towns or garrisons at least, this was structured along Roman lines to include initial rituals with incense and wine libations, followed by the killing of the sacrificial beast and distribution of its meat. The many finds of animal figurines may represent substitute sacrifices for living animals, while miniature or model weapons and tools also may replace their real counterparts in offerings.

Above left: Hoard of votive material from near Bury St Edmunds. (SF-D4-D044)

Above right: Spearhead inscribed with a vow to Silvanus, south Cambs. (LEIC-35DO1B)

Two images of Minerva, the most frequently represented female deity in Britain, illustrate the diverse ways gods were imagined in the statues which were created of them. A copper alloy statuette from Hailey, a sinuous figure 170 mm high, closely copies its Greco-Roman models. The helmet of the goddess, pushed up to reveal her face and parted hair, las lost its crest. Draped in a *chiton* (long tunic) and cloak, Minerva wears on her left arm a goatskin *aegis* (protective cover) carrying the petrifying features of Medusa, with its curling edges and the coiling snakes of the gorgon's hair reproduced in fine detail. The (missing) left hand may have held a shield, the right probably a spear or sceptre. The rivets at the shoulders, to represent the brooches fastening her tunic, are the best preserved of the silver details which embellished the figure, in gleaming contrast with the bronze. The figure of the goddess is revealed beneath layers of fabric, thicker for her cloak and finer for her tunic. In contrast the small lead alloy figure from Tidbury Green re-imagines Minerva as a naked equestrian figure. The crested helmet identifies her as the daughter of Jupiter, but the legs splayed as if straddling a horse and the nudity of the lower body, with genitalia clearly indicated, do not follow Roman models.

Above left: Minerva figurine, Hayley, 170 mm high.

Above right: Equestrian Minerva figurine, Tidbury Green, Warks. (WAW-C54295)

Images of Mars, found in abundance in eastern and south-west England, tell a similar story. A statuette from Stanstead Abbotts closely follows classical models. Worn but finely made, this small figurine probably held a spear in its missing right hand. With a crested helmet pushed up from his face, the god wears a square-necked cuirass, crossed by a baldric (sword belt) with a kilt below, and a cloak hanging from the left shoulder. The left arm is empty, and there is little space for the shield it might once have held. The face is worn, but luxuriant hair curls out from beneath his Corinthian helmet. Another form of the god, particular to Britain, puts Mars on a galloping horse. In an example from Stow-cum-Quy purchased by the British Museum, a cloak billows out behind the god, whose right arm once held a spear. With ears pricked up, plaited mane and decorated harness, the horse is a fitting mount to carry its divine rider. Many small enamelled brooches copy the same figure, especially in large numbers (ninety-five) at Bosworth, Leicestershire, where a Roman temple has been identified on the battlefield where Richard III met his end. In rural Britain Mars was more likely worshipped as a defender of crops than as a war god.

Mars figurine, Stansted Abbots,
84 mm high.

Horse and rider (Mars) figurine, Stow-cum-Quy. (SF-99E3E4)

Horse and rider brooch, with
enamelling, Bosworth, Leics.
(LEIC-9A25C1)

Usually, finds of statuary occur in isolation but detecting on the Severn floodplain near Gloucester in 2017 brought to light a group of objects buried as scrap: 5 kg of copper alloy, amongst which are fragments of statues and offering boxes. The only complete piece is a small dog standing alert, head raised, ears pricked up and tongue extended to bark a challenge. The lips and muscles are curiously stylised, especially the leaf-like haunches. Amongst the fragments are parts of a statue of Diana, goddess of hunting, including a lappet (decorative piece) from a boot in the form of a bear skin. The dog may once have been part of a statue group in which the goddess was accompanied by hounds. Another fragment, this time of an inscription on thin sheet bronze, appears to refer to a collection of money (*conlatio*) to fund a statue. These may be remnants of the treasures of a temple closed in the fourth century AD as the pagan cults of the Roman colony at Gloucester dissolved.

Figurine of a dog, near Gloucester, 214 mm long. (Photograph by Eve Andreski)

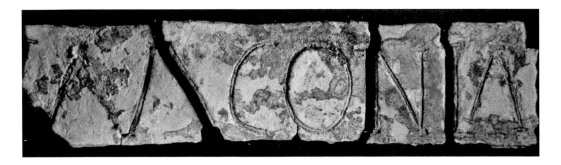

Bronze inscription, from 'near Gloucester' hoard (GLO-BE1187). (Photograph by Eve Andreski)

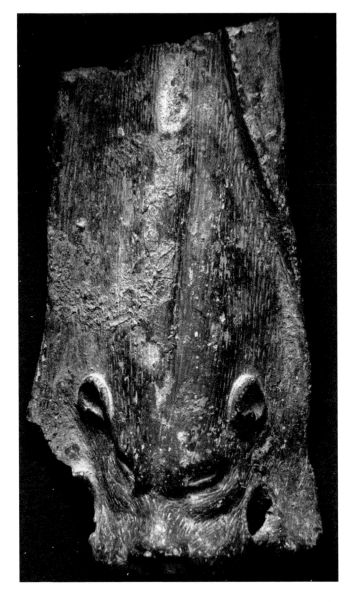

Copper alloy boot upper from statue of Diana, 'near Gloucester' hoard (GLO-BE1187). (Photograph by Eve Andreski)

Images of less common gods demonstrate the diversity of Roman religion. A copper alloy figurine from Burrington takes the shape of the zodiac sign Capricorn, the hybrid goat and fish, with forelegs outstretched and body tapering to a tail fin. Fur is hatched on the face and forelimbs, with scales on the rest. Metal figures of Capricorn (and other Zodiac signs) are rare finds. Figures found in Germany and Austria have sockets for attachment as vehicle or furniture fittings, but the Burrington figure sits on its flattened underside. Capricorn is associated in antiquity with the emperor Augustus, who chose it as his star sign for its symbolism of solar rebirth at the winter solstice as well as its hybrid terrestrial and marine nature, expressing dominion over land and sea. Its imperial association made it an emblem of the 2nd Legion Augusta, based at Caerleon, across the Bristol Channel from the figurine's find-spot.

The sun god himself, Sol, is identifiable from his radiating crown on a vessel mount from Lidgate, perhaps re-used as an offering. A copper alloy figurine found near the fort at Newton Kyme also connects to a solar deity. Clad in cloak, trousers and Phrygian cap, with lowered torch, signifying darkness, this is a unique image in metal of Cautopates, attendant of the god Mithras. Stone images of him are typically placed in Mithras sanctuaries opposite his companion, Cautes, bringer of light.

Capricorn figurine, Burrington, 250 mm long and weighing almost 900 g. (© Somerset County Council and South West Heritage Trust, 2019)

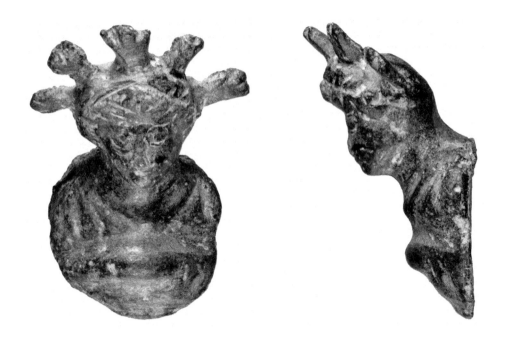

Vessel mount in the form of Sol Invictus, Lidgate, Suffolk. (SF-896782)

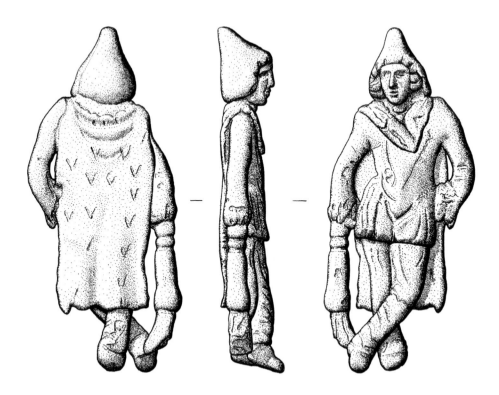

Figurine of Cautopates, Newton Kyme, North Yorks. (SWYOR-9FCBB3) (Drawing by Dominic Andrews)

The principle element of ritual was sacrifice, connecting gods and men through shared consumption of a slaughtered animal. Model animals were substitutes for real victims or additional offerings. One such copper alloy figurine from Holbrook shows a muscular bull with two unusual characteristics. In the centre of its head is the stump of a third horn, perhaps identifying this bull as a manifestation of a local deity. However, wrapped around its body is a *dorsuale*, a cloth band reserving an animal for sacrifice. Bulls in peak condition like this one are often shown garlanded as they approach the *victimarius* (killer of sacrificial animals) in scenes on Roman public monuments. The plumage of a cockerel figurine from Cople, another likely sacrificial substitute, is vividly coloured in red, blue and green enamel inlay.

At Pentridge the hand of a copper alloy figurine, broken at the wrist, illustrates another stage of sacrifice. It holds an incense box (*acerra*), its lid raised to reveal heaped-up frankincense within. The hand might be of a priest, probably dressed in a toga with a fold pulled over his head. Along with music and libations of wine, burning incense invited the god to the sacrificial feast.

Bull figurine, Holbrook, 61 mm long.

Enamel
|||||| Blue
|///// Green

0   5 cm

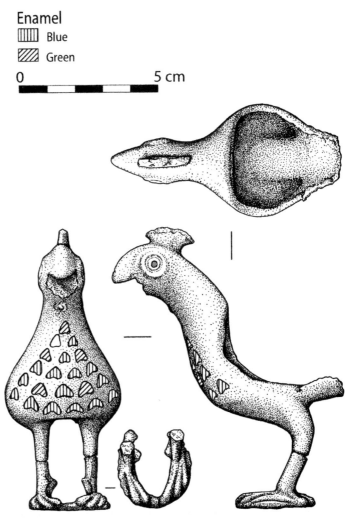

Enamelled figure
in the form of a
cockerel from Cople,
Beds. (SOM-745EA2)
(Drawing by
M. Trevarthen)

Hand with incense
box, Pentridge, Dorset.
(DOR-8C6C09)

Some figurines will have had inscribed bases, naming gods and dedicators. No examples survive from the PAS but other instances of Latin prayers do. They record the fulfilment of the contract-like vow made by the dedicator to thank the god with an offering, once the god had acted on their behalf. The famous 'leaf' plaques for the goddess Senuna from Ashwell, Herts, carry dedications of this kind. A fragment of a copper alloy plaque from the Thames foreshore provides another example. Incised in well-made capitals, it preserves part of a dedication to Bona Dea, a deity rarely met outside Italy, and to the spirits (*numina*) of the emperors, made by a Pannonian (from the area of modern-day Hungary) who records in the final line that he fulfilled his vow. This dedication and those to Senuna were written on purpose-made plaques, displayed in temples. Recent discoveries from a shrine in south Cambridgeshire show the use of expedient media for messages, including a dedication to Mars dot-punched onto a possible harness fitting.

Above left: Votive plaque, Thames foreshore, 72 mm long.

Above right: Mount dedicated to Mars, south Cambs. (LEIC-A9ED3D)

Sacrifice required prior purification. This is one function of the many metal jugs and pans documented by the PAS, which served to clean the hands of participants. The enigmatic lead tank found at Preshute also probably served a purifying purpose, but for the whole body. The preserved fragments are parts of several panels joined to a flat circular base to form a cylindrical vessel. These panels were decorated with 'straps' of herringbone motifs which sometimes masked joins between panels. This is one of thirty such tanks known from Britain, dated to the fourth century AD and later, most between 0.5 and 1 m in diameter and with sides up to 0.6 m high. The chi-rho motif (or Christogram) – the first letters of Christ's name in Greek – on some tanks identifies them as immersion vessels for Christian baptism, but others might serve for any cult as part of ritualised cleansing or initiation. Few objects with clear Christian affiliation have been recorded by the PAS. Other than coins of the short-lived usurper-emperor Magnentius (AD 350–53), the only Christogram so far documented is cut on the bezel of a copper alloy ring from Narborough.

Above: Fragments of lead tank, Preshute, *c.* 950 mm long, 300 mm high.

Right: Bezel of copper alloy finger ring with Christogram, Narborough, Leics. (LEIC-5FC533)

Nummus of the emperor Magnentius with Christogram, AD 352–53, Trier mint, Wilberfoss, East Riding. (NLM-A08783)

Chapter 4
Luck and Magic

The Preshute tank (No. 14) also carried a phallic motif cast on one panel, a symbol found on many Roman objects. Whether this excludes a Christian use in this case is difficult to say, and perforations around the phallus perhaps suggest an attempt to 'kill' its power. But the phallus is the most common motif among the symbols, auspicious, fearsome or grotesque, sometimes ridiculous, used to repel the pervasive effects of *Invidia*, or the Evil Eye. This diversity is nicely illustrated on a repoussé gold sheet from Keswick and Intwood, a pendant perhaps, on which *Invidia* manifested as a central eye is assaulted by multiple adversaries, weapons, clawed animals and phalluses. Such symbols proliferated as Roman Britons used apotropaic images, drawn from long-lived Mediterranean traditions, to provide supernatural protection outside the formal context of ritual. Charms were worn on the bodies of humans and animals. They were also applied to inanimate entities, such as vehicles or buildings, for similar purposes. For example the bridge abutment at Chesters, on Hadrian's Wall, was carved with a phallus for protection against the North Tyne in spate, while the phallus on the antler roundel from Dowgate, London, also drew on the virile potency of the stag (and the medical properties ascribed to antler) to increase its power.

Images of the gods themselves also served as protective figures in this life or the next: Priapus with his emblematic phallus, for instance, or lucky Fortune herself. The many divine images from intaglios (carved stones) set into finger rings reveal that all gods could serve this protective purpose in objects worn on the body. Writing, too, was employed for the same ends. PAS discoveries have included magical texts in the form of written charms and invocations. Occasionally, too, there are instances of the aggressive use of magic. For example, a curse tablet from Lidgate, Suffolk (SF-BA1337), seeking vengeance for the theft of rings, uses the same principles as the curses from Bath to harm the thief.

Evil Eye amulet, Keswick and Intwood, Norfolk. (NMS-B9A004)

Phallus carved on a bridge abutment at Chesters, Hadrian's Wall. (Carole Raddato, used under Creative Commons licence CC BY SA 2.0)

Antler roundel, Dowgate, London. (LON-791EC5)

Formerly thought to be worn by Roman soldiers, PAS examples show phallic amulets in fact widely used as protective symbols in the Romano-British countryside. The particular power of the phallic image is difficult to pin down, a symbol of fear (through aggression), fertility and fun, the latter especially through strange juxtapositions with other motifs (No. 16). The copper alloy phallus from Higham, with a loop to allow suspension, is likely to have been one such amulet. In other examples the use of gold, associated with the sun, lent the propitious power of this material to the device. A gold ring from Wing, with a tiny phallic motif on its bezel, was so small that it could only have been worn by a small child. Indeed, grave finds confirm that such rings and pendants were worn from a young age by children, especially vulnerable to ill fortune. Phallic images could also protect the bodies of animals, as a harness pendant from Piercebridge shows, modelled in the form of male genitals.

Above left: Copper alloy phallic pendant, Higham, 52 mm long.

Above right: Gold finger ring with phallus on bezel, Wing, Bucks. (BUC-C9CEE4)

Harness pendant with suspension
loop, Piercebridge. (BH-F31E4C)

Phallic images amplified their apotropaic power by placing the phallus in puzzling or incongruous combinations, such as giving it a pair of wings. The copper alloy amulet from Rushden is a good example of such incongruity. At first sight it might be taken for a genre scene, a bird feeding on berries, as is sometimes carved into intaglios for finger rings. This, however, is a pecker of a different kind. The bird, a crow perhaps, grips a phallus rather than a branch with its claws. Its beak tugs at one of the testes, jerking it sharply upwards. It is not quite clear how the object was to be used – suspended as a pendant, perhaps, using the loop made where the claws join the phallus. The double-take prompted by the pairing of bird and phallus has the potential to mislead the viewer, reinforcing the power of the charm to avert ill fortune.

A famous example of this incongruity is the *tintinnabulum* (wind chime) from Herculaneum on which the phallus metamorphoses into a dog and turns back to fight the gladiator to whom it belongs. A copper alloy amulet from Longford provides a different example of this belligerent potency. Where the head of this quadruped should be, a phallus projects instead, replacing the horns or teeth of the real animal in aggressive defence of the body or object to which this amulet was attached.

The Rushden pecker, 30 mm long.

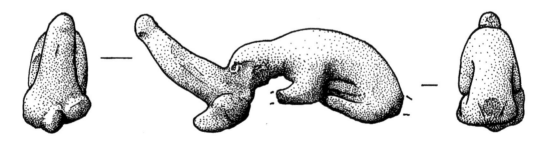

Quadruped with phallus head, Longford, Derbyshire. (DENO-82D537) (Drawing by David Williams)

Phallic images have a special association with the god Priapus which helps to explain their power. Priapus was a divine protector of gardens and orchards; in the verses known as the *Priapeia*, a speaking wooden statue of the god threatens the rape of any would-be thief or scrumper. Representations of Priapus are rare in Britain, though there is a small cluster in Essex and Suffolk, of which the figurine from Thorrington is one. The turbanned and bearded god hoists his tunic to show an erect phallus, on either side of which dangle bunches of grapes, emblems of the fruitfulness he oversaw. The nearby colony at Colchester may explain the presence of a god better documented in Italy, especially one with such careful modeling of anatomy and clothing. However, the PAS also reveals likely local equivalents in Britain, statuettes where the facial features, clothing and limbs all play second fiddle to oversized genitals. Figurines from Cawood and Ripon, respectively cast in copper and lead alloy, illustrate these much cruder fertility figures.

Priapus figurine, Thorrington, 80 mm tall.

Left: Lead alloy Priapic figurine, Cawood. (SWYOR-A153A2)

Right: Lead alloy Priapic figurine, North Yorks. (YORYM-B3FE27)

Through their association with fertility, female genitalia also commonly feature as apotropaic images. The most common example is the so-called 'coffee-bean' stud, a fitting for horse harnesses. Excavated examples have been documented at many auxiliary forts but so many have been recorded by PAS from the Romano-British countryside (more than sixty) that their exclusive use on soldiers' riding equipment is in doubt. An example from Little Laver illustrates their usual form. The small fitting comprises a hexagonal plate carrying an oval boss with a slot running its length (the 'coffee bean'). Beneath the plate are prongs which push through the leather harness strap. Some examples also have a loop for suspending a pendant, for instance from Upham, or a more elaborate leaf-like plate, as at West Rudham. Like other images of male and female genitalia, the 'coffee bean' or vulvate decoration on the boss gives the stud a protective force as well as a practical purpose, preserving the well-being of the horse wearing the harness. The same vulvate image also sometimes features on brooches and rings.

Left: Coffee bean mount, Little Laver, 27 mm long.

Below left: Vulvate mount from Upham, Hants. (HAMP3503)

Below right: Vulvate mount from West Rudham, Norfolk. (NMS-30C9B2)

Fortuna was the common recipient of soldiers' prayers in Britain to protect them from the arbitrary whims of fate. A military connection may explain the presence of this small diademed figure of the goddess near the garrison at Piercebridge. The figurine can be identified from the cornucopia (horn of plenty) held in the crook of her left arm. The overflowing fruit shows the favour she might bring, while there are traces by her right foot of the rudder with which she steered fate. Other statues of Fortuna also include a wheel, symbolising luck's ever-changing character. The tiny cornucopia cut in an intaglio (carved stone) set in a gold ring from Newton Valence illustrates the borrowing of Fortuna's favour as a protective device worn on the body. Soldiers would also have known the goddess on coins which showed how the emperor's good character (*virtus*) promoted the good fortune of the Roman state. For example, a denarius from Ashwell (AD 103–111) labels the reigning emperor Trajan as the best of princes (*optimus princeps*) in the legend which surrounds an elegant Fortuna with rudder and cornucopia.

Figurine of Fortuna, Gainford area, 60 mm high.

Cornucopia on intaglio, Newton Valence, Hants. (HAMP-2B06D9)

Fortuna, reverse of denarius of Trajan, Ashwell, Herts. (BH-FDC6BB)

20. Phylactery or charm for safe childbirth (BERK-0B671 2007T1), AD 200–400, south Oxfordshire.

The PAS has been productive in charms for ensuring good health in moments of collective danger, such as plague, or individual peril. Combining the power of its auspicious material, gold, with its magical text, is one such amulet from south Oxfordshire, guarding against the risks of childbirth. Written on a wafer-thin sheet or *lamella*, this amulet carried sixteen lines, starting with magical characters and the 'holy names' of mysterious divinities, followed by an appeal in Greek to these names for protection of Fabia, daughter of Terentia, during her pregnancy. Although the symbols and formulas echo others from the Roman world, a protective charm or phylactery of this specific sort is not otherwise recorded before the sixth century AD. When completed the charm was rolled into a tight cylinder and was probably worn round the neck in a case like the thin tube found at Easton Constantine. The ribbed gold leaf plaque from Lewes, a medical offering seemingly in the form of a uterus, was probably also offered to obtain divine help for good health or reproduction. It too is a first from Britain.

Phylactery, south Oxfordshire, 63 mm long, 28.3 mm wide.

Amulet case, Eaton Constantine, Salop. (HESH-21275B)

Gold leaf plaque, in form of uterus, Lewes, E. Sussex. (SUSS-0F1783)

Amulets also used animal images to apply a protective power. The myriad of lions decorating all kinds of objects clearly come from Greco-Roman art, but other animals have a local echo, above all the wild boar, an apt image for its power and aggression. One distinctive object using a boar image is a copper alloy amulet for the yoke of draught animals, illustrated by an example from Great Canfield. It comprises two main elements: a boar's head with a gaping mouth and a large tusk which projects from the back of the head. In other examples of the same object a real tooth is used instead of a copper alloy tusk. The boar occurs too on copper alloy plate brooches of the second and third century AD. On an example from Willingdon and Jevington, complete apart from the pin, the curving snout and bristling mane are emphasised in the boar's strong profile. The colour contrast – white metal coating on the mane, green enamel for the body and eye – gives the swine extra flair. From the same parish comes a local reminder of the significance of boar for Iron Age societies, in the form of a small stylised figurine.

Amulet, Great Canfield, Essex, 106 mm long.

Boar brooch, Willingdon and Jevington, E. Sussex. (SUSS-DB2C32)

Boar figurine,
Willingdon
and Jevington.
(SUSS-6F88D3)

Chapter 5
Dressing the Body

After coins, dress accessories and jewellery are the most numerous items documented by the PAS, and above all brooches. More than 2,000 are recorded annually, which are classified by archaeologists depending on the shape of their bow or plate. As well as other dress fasteners, including belts and button-and-loop fasteners, items to adorn hair and body also survive in thousands of examples, finger rings, bracelets, hair pins, earrings and neck rings. These objects demonstrate major features of provincial Roman society; for example, the use of appearance to mark belonging to a community or to express difference in social status.

The sheer number and variety of brooches with bows, dress fastenings which proliferated in late Iron Age northern Europe, reveal the continuing importance of indigenous dress style. Funerary portraits are a key source for showing how brooches were used in regional costumes, especially by women, all with the common characteristic of using paired brooches (and sometimes more) to pin tube-like tunics at the shoulders. The head stud brooches found near Market Weighton are still linked with the chain which connected them from one shoulder to the other, perhaps because they had been buried together in a hoard or grave.

The regional clustering of many brooch types also makes it clear when 'alien' brooches are found far from home. Even if the precise story behind any one brooch cannot be reconstructed, their function to pin clothing puts them among the intimate personal effects of their individual owners as they moved across the empire, though brooches were also traded in their own right. Variation in size, materials, motifs and techniques also makes clear how status (and other) differences were advertised through the adornment of the body. Given their close connection to the person of the wearer, ornament was also well-suited to carry the protective images discussed in Chapter 4.

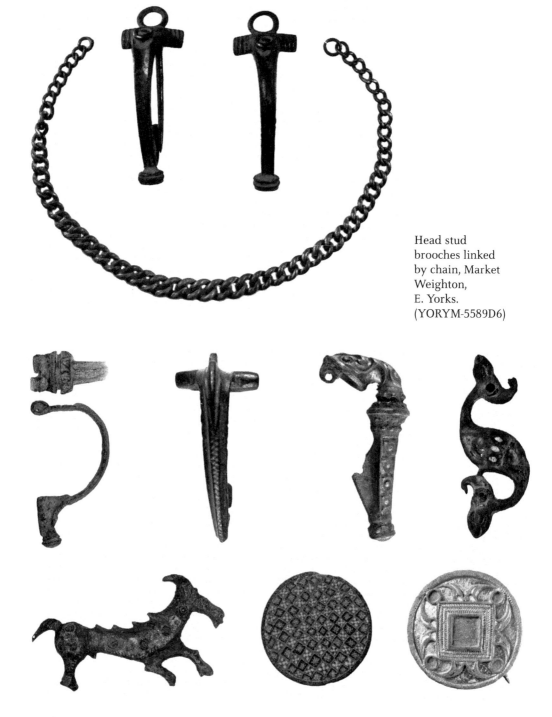

Head stud brooches linked by chain, Market Weighton, E. Yorks. (YORYM-5589D6)

Brooches of the first to third century, in chronological order, top left to bottom right (not to scale): WILT-316C6A, BUC-401B71, LVPL-180D95, LANCUM-B56813, LEIC-D80772, LVPL-F1F6CC, HAMP-58BF76.

The Polden Hill brooch is one of many brooch types dated to the first and second centuries AD, named after one of the first discoveries in Somerset. A well-preserved copper alloy example from Astley and Dunley shows some typical characteristics, including a hump-like bow and the flattened ends or 'caps' of the wings which house the spring. However, its decoration is exceptional, including its ridged bow with rows of bosses on either side and an elaborately moulded foot. It also retains traces of silvering on the head and catchplate. The Polden Hill brooch from West Knoyle has extra mouldings by the head, indicating that it belongs to the sub-group of these brooches from Somerset, Wiltshire and Gloucestershire.

Polden Hill brooches are so far attested in PAS records by more than 2,700 examples. Their distribution exemplifies the regional character of many brooch types. Although found across Britain, there is a very high concentration along the River Severn and throughout the West Midlands, as far north as Staffordshire and Shropshire. These brooches are not an identity badge for a particular group as this concentration spans several communities, including the colony of veterans at Gloucester and the *civitates* (city states) of the Dobunni and Cornovii. These finds represent the output of many artisans making brooches within a shared tradition, working the towns, fairs and markets along the main routes of western Britain.

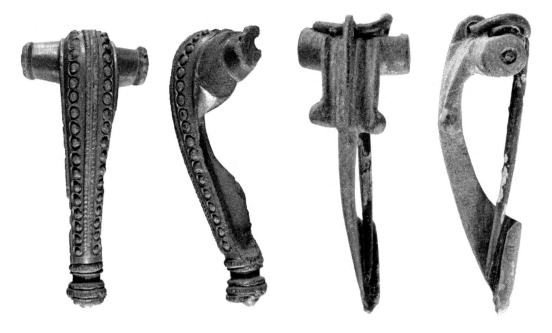

Above left: Polden Hill brooch, Astley and Dunley, 55 mm long.

Above right: Polden Hill brooch, West Knoyle, Wilts. (SOM-8100BB)

53

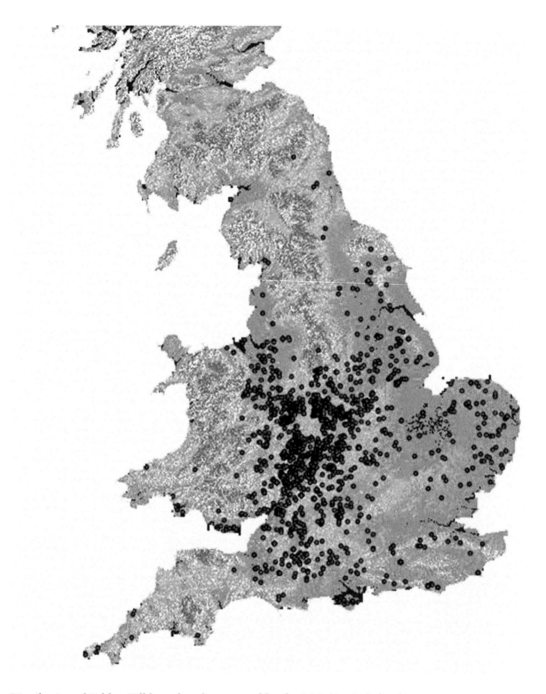

Distribution of Polden Hill brooches documented by the PAS. (Angie Bolton)

A copper alloy openwork brooch, found on the Isle of Wight, nicely illustrates the likely movement of people attested through dress objects. The brooch has a flat frame within which is a monogram formed by three letters, R, M and A, or R(o)ma. On the back are remnants of pin and catch-plate.

This is the first discovery from Britain of a brooch of this form, dated to the later second and earlier third centuries AD. It is otherwise mainly found in garrisons and settlements along the River Danube. Roma is probably Dea Roma, the deity personifying the city of Rome. Metalwork worn by Roman soldiers often uses this openwork style (e.g. No. 7) and includes images of Dea Roma, Mars or the she-wolf and twin boys Romulus and Remus. These evoke Rome's military traditions and invite the god to protect the body of the soldier. No garrison has yet been identified on the Isle of Wight, though the fort at Portchester, occupied from the later third century onwards, lies north-east across the Solent. Wight's location on a busy cross-Channel route may explain the presence of the Roma brooch, perhaps brought by a soldier moving from a Danubian garrison to Britain.

If read from right to left, the monogram instead reads as Am(o)r, or 'love'. The puzzle offered by decipherment of the monogram was perhaps a further deterrent to a malign gaze (see No. 16). A puzzle of a different kind is presented by another brooch from Orton, carrying the text, '*Si amas*', 'if you love...' asking the reader to imagine the rest.

Above left: Roma monogram brooch, west of Newport, 34 mm diameter.

Above right: Disc brooch with motto 'SI A/MAS', Orton, Northants. (WMID-746CF7)

Other brooches also hint at the movement of their wearers to Britain from other parts of the empire. Like the Roma brooch, some are more typical of the Danube provinces. One such is the small copper alloy *Ankerfibel*, so-called from its anchor-shaped foot, from South Darley. Also dated to the second and third centuries AD, this type is documented in more than 200 instances from north-eastern Italy through the Danube provinces to the Black Sea but is a rare find in Britain. A zoomorphic brooch from Dodcott cum Wilkesley is also best paralleled along the Danube. It shows a horse walking left with head lowered as if grazing. Traces of white metal coating survive. The closest documented parallels are specifically in Pannonia, i.e. modern Hungary.

The red and blue enamelled copper alloy plate brooch with crescent head and animal foot from St Margaret at Cliffe represents contact with less distant areas. Of a type rarely documented in Britain, it belongs to type II of the 'Groupe de Lille' second-century brooches, found in Gaul and the Rhineland.

Ankerfibel, South Darley, 40 mm long.

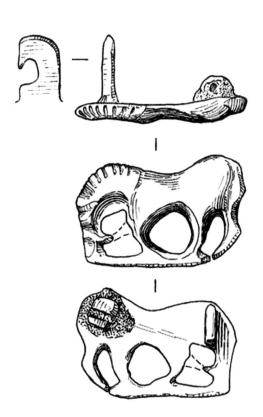

Above: Horse brooch, Dodcott cum Wilkesley, Cheshire. (LVPL-2092E5) (Drawing by David Williams)

Right: 'Groupe de Lille' brooch, St Margaret at Cliffe, Kent. (KENT-82B1A6)

Copper alloy button and loop fasteners, dated to the first and second centuries AD, fastened clothing and/or smaller pieces of horse harness. Typically 30–40 mm long where complete, they comprise a button-like head with a shank projecting at the back, bent at 90 degrees to form an offset circular or triangular loop. In 1970, when the major study of these was published, 165 examples were known; since 1997 more than 460 have been documented by the PAS, mainly in northern England and the north-east Midlands but also across the rest of England and the Welsh marches. Fasteners of this type have often been excavated on military sites, but so many new examples from the countryside suggest their frequent use by civilians too. The elaborate chequerboard enamelling on the tear-drop-shaped button of this fastener from Holme-on-Spalding-Moor echoes a decorative style used locally on Iron Age and early Roman weapons and harness. Another East Yorkshire find from Cottam is more typical of such fasteners, also drop-shaped but without enamelling. An Isle of Wight fastener, by contrast, has a double head with coral bosses.

Button and loop fastener,
Holme-upon-Spalding-Moor,
43 mm long.

Button and
loop fastener,
Cottam, E. Yorks.
(YORYM-604C99)

Button and loop fastener, Isle of Wight. (IOW-070B4E)

A fourth-century finger ring from Tangley illustrates the sophistication of gold rings from the province. The bezel and hoop have separated on one side but the ring is otherwise complete, with spirals of gold filigree on its wide shoulders. The intaglio setting depicts a winged male figure, leaning on a pillar and a flaming torch (?) – perhaps the god Mercury. Later in date is a silver ring from Nether Wallop, one of fifty-four known as the 'Brancaster type' after the fort on the Norfolk coast where the ring type was first documented, dated to the final decades of Roman rule. The bezel image is one of the most vivid, a spiral of chevrons forming a tightly coiled serpent, either a Greco-Roman sea-dragon or a 'wyrm' from Germanic myth. A second or third-century ring from Broomfield is more typical in respect of its materials (copper alloy) and plain facetted hoop. However, the short text it carries – *veni futuve*, 'come and fuck', a woman's invitation to a sexual partner – is so far unparalleled.

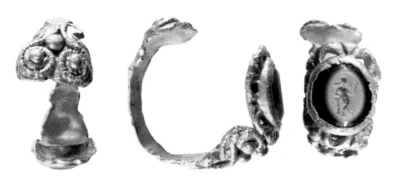

Gold ring, Tangley, 22 mm diameter, weight 5.6 g.

Silver ring, Nether Wallop, Hants. (WILT-17E7E6; 2017T431)

Copper alloy ring, Broomfield, Essex. (ESS-887174)

Of more than 2,000 bracelets and their fragments (mostly the latter) recorded by Finds Liaison Officers, fewer than forty are made of silver and fewer than ten of gold, indicative of restricted access to precious metals according to means. A second- or third-century silver bracelet made from a tightly spiralled tube of silver wire from the Dalton area illustrates the complexity of some Roman jewellery, paralleled in examples in gold from Egypt and a silvered bronze from the Rhineland. Each terminal is enclosed in a tubular collar decorated with a filigree wire in meander form. Hinges connected the now broken terminals to the silver-sheet bezel. The upper face of the latter is decorated with herringbone, formed from twisted wire, around a central raised setting for an oval gem which has dropped out of position. Engraved into its translucent orange-red surface is a seated Jupiter, sceptre in his left hand and *patera* (shallow pan) in his right, about to pour a libation on a flaming altar. The copper alloy snake-head bracelet from Itchen Valley, so-called because of the shape of its terminals, is a much more typical find.

Above left: Silver bracelet, Dalton area, 80 mm x 61 mm hoop.

Above right: Snake head bracelet, Itchen Valley, Hants. (HAMP-11A268)

Around ninety Roman earrings have been documented by the PAS, most being simple copper alloy penannular hoops. More elaborate examples in gold again illustrate how bodily adornment could convey the wealth of those who wore it. A late first- to early second-century AD piece from Stagsden exemplifies the complex decoration on gold earrings. The main decoration comprises a sheet gold crescent, carrying applied filigree wire. A rilled wire (i.e. a wire cut with repeated tiny channels) runs around the sheet's edge, with each crescent terminal decorated with a single gold bead. The inner field is decorated with thinner spirals of rilled wire in a symmetrical arrangement. Originally, the spiral ends were set with green glass beads, one of which survives intact. The attachment consists of a double loop, soldered to the back of the sheet and holding a ring of gold wire. Although there is no obvious way of attaching the earring to the earlobe, finds of similar rings in graves confirm its function. As a lunar symbol associated with the goddess Diana, female reproduction and lunar light, the crescent decoration also offered its fortune-enhancing quality to the wearer.

Gold earring, Stagsden, 32 mm long.

Chapter 6
Styling the Body

Like clothes and jewellery, the body itself could communicate the identity of the sitter. Definitions of 'clean' and 'dirty' changed, with a complex repertoire of tools evolving for manipulating the personal appearance of women and men, combining elements of Iron Age and Roman practice. The development of these habits was closely linked to personal status, since the tools, raw materials and time for modifying appearance sometimes depended on the labour of others, including assistance from slaves or servants. The most obvious innovation was bathing, a habit which in Roman eyes differentiated Roman from barbarian; in the same description where he flagged the Britons' adoption of the toga, Tacitus also reported their fondness for the pleasures of urban life, including bathing. This is no empty rhetoric: bathhouses can be found everywhere, in towns, villas and above all garrisons, for exercise and comfort. The objects once used for cleaning or cutting of skin, hair, nails, teeth and so on reveal the emphasis put on grooming. More than 600 nail cleaners, for example, have been documented to date by the PAS, spread widely across eastern and southern England. Similarly, tools for preparing and applying materials to the body, including cosmetics and perfumed oils, have survived from the same regions. Recent work on Roman burials has detected some of the sweet-smelling substances used by Roman Britons, at least applied to the bodies of the dead. Among the aromatic resins so far identified is frankincense from Yemen, a token of the distance travelled by some cosmetic materials and perfumes, and the associated expense. On the handle of a small knife from Dodderhill, likely used for grooming, the goddess Venus models the perfect form as the desired end result of all this labour, while the Longdon Neptune shows the counterpart male physique, sculpted by bathhouse exercise.

Above left: Knife handle in form of 'modest' Venus, Dodderhill, Worcs. (WAW-378661)

Above right: Neptune figurine, Longdon, Worcs. (GLO-082F26)

Individual mortars are quite common finds; complete cosmetic sets with pestle and mortar like this one from Shotesham are rarer. Not found outside Britain, use of these objects began in the late Iron Age and spread during Roman rule. Their purpose was probably to grind minerals for cosmetic use, either as skin powder or eye shadow. Like other sets, this finely cast and engraved mortar and pestle mirror each other in their form. The pestle, with a rounded keel, is of 'rocking-horse' type, with a high centre-loop on struts. At either end of the mortar is a stylised cattle head, and the hatched bow has a trefoil loop plate below. This find was discovered close to those of other examples of the same type in north Norfolk. The bovine heads at either end, as well as the possible sexual connotation of the pestle within the mortar, lend appropriate protective symbolism to objects which created materials to apply to the body's boundaries and which were probably kept close to the person, suspended from their loops.

Pestle and mortar,
Shotesham, mortar
57 mm long.

Among other small tools for intimate grooming, tweezers, nail cleaners and ear scoops are commonly documented instruments. Usually these are found as separate items, but an example from Leafield illustrates the sets which occasionally survive. The tweezers comprise a single piece of metal, folded to create two parallel plates with curved ends for gripping. The ear scoop has a rounded shaft which flattens and expands into a tiny spoon. The nail cleaner, another object not used outside Britain, had a leaf-shape blade with a forked terminal. All three ended in loops for suspending them from a simple metal hoop. In some cases, these suites of objects were suspended from a châtelaine brooch, i.e. a type of plate brooch with a bar from which the instruments could hang. An example from North Kesteven represents a well-preserved common type, with a rectangular panel beneath and arch above, decorated with blue, red and yellow enamel. A lug for the pin and catchplate survive behind, but the suspension bar beneath is lost. Occasionally this suite of tools has been found with cosmetic sets (see No. 29), suggesting that they might have been used in the same grooming routine, by both men and women.

Above left: Toilet instruments, Leafield, tweezers 64 mm long.

Above right: Enamelled châtelaine, North Kesteven, Lincs. (LIN-A40146)

Fashions in shaving varied significantly over time. From the clean-shaven figures of the first century AD, funerary portraits of the second and third centuries show private individuals emulating the fashion set by the emperor Hadrian and his successors to grow ever longer beards. Among the artefacts identified as razors, one type has a knife of trapezoidal form, with a cutting edge on each side, held by a small zoomorphic handle. Of the six examples recorded by the PAS the razor from Bishopstoke is the most complete. Its triangular copper alloy handle takes the form of a griffin's head, with small beak and ears, and incisions to mark the eyes and plumage/fur. The iron blade was secured through a slot in the handle and two iron rivets, a little of it remaining between two transverse mouldings. A small copper alloy knife from Southill, 95 mm long, illustrates another type of likely razor, with a short broad blade with a curving cutting edge, and a thin handle with a trefoil terminal, pierced perhaps to allow suspension.

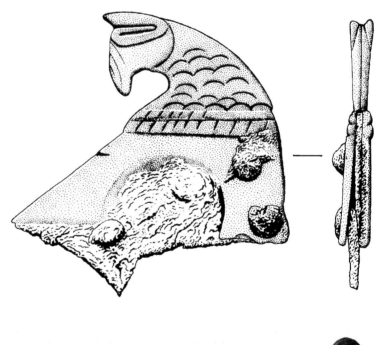

Razor handle,
Bishopstoke,
22 mm long.
(Drawing by Alan
Cracknell)

Short-handled
razor, Southill,
Beds. (BH-FBD78C)

Other small knives with folding or fixed blades and handles in human and animal form served for shaving, grooming and toilette. One extraordinary type, now documented in four cases, shows three naked individuals in an erotic tangle. The details are a little obscured by corrosion, but the most recent example from Mappleborough Green shows its typical features. A standing man leans backwards, seemingly having sex with a woman whose legs are tucked under his arms. She perches on the shoulders of a smaller naked male who kneels beneath her. Little survives of the iron blade, buried in a slot in the standing figure's back. This scene from the Roman theatre combines acrobatics, sex (real or simulated) and farce too, given the riskiness of the configuration.

Two other examples illustrate the variety of forms these toilet knives could take. One well-preserved handle from the Tees at Piercebridge takes the form of a lower left leg, with the stitching of the sock and the footwear modelled in detail. The tusks of a wild boar-shaped handle from Ditchingham are a (jokey) reminder of the sharpness of the blade folded into the pig's underside. Fierce, curious and comical images were appropriate to a cutting object used on the body's boundaries where symbolic protection might be needed.

Toilet knife,
Mappleborough
Green, 66.4 mm long.

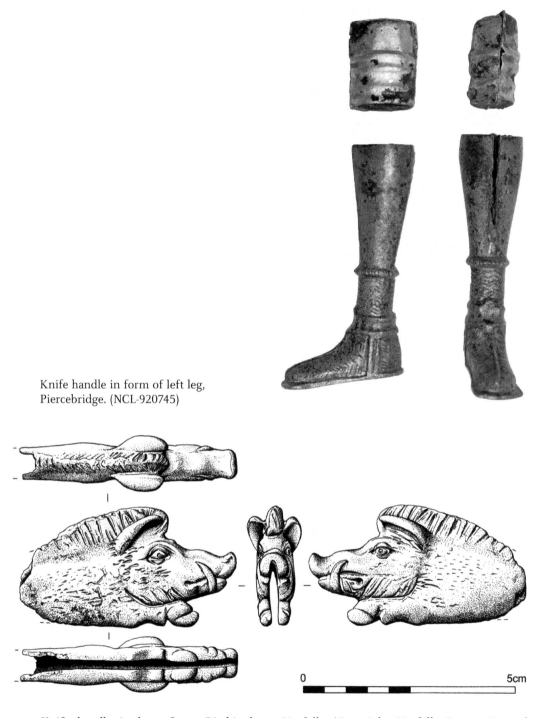

Knife handle in form of left leg, Piercebridge. (NCL-920745)

Knife handle in boar form, Ditchingham, Norfolk. (Copyright Norfolk County Council Environment Service. Illustration by Sue White)

0   5cm

The mirror is a key component of the new tools and practices for modifying personal appearance which emerged in the late Iron Age. A copper alloy mirror dating to the last century of the Iron Age found in plough-spread fragments at Bromham is typical of the type found in (mainly) female high-status graves around the time of the Roman conquest. Conservation at Verulamium Museum shows the mirror to have a three-lobed 'lyre' arrangement engraved on its 1-mm-thick surface. The swirling outlines enclose zones of 'basketry' hatching, contrasting with smooth blank metal around them. The looped handle ends in openwork attachments into which the plate slotted, held in place by rivets. As well as smaller copper alloy mirrors, lead-framed mirrors are also documented in the Roman period. An example from north Bedfordshire carries a Greek text around the setting for the glass, recording that it was made in the workshop of Quintus Likinios Touteinos in Arles. The aperture is so small in this and other lead-framed mirrors that they have been thought to have been made as offerings rather than as functional objects.

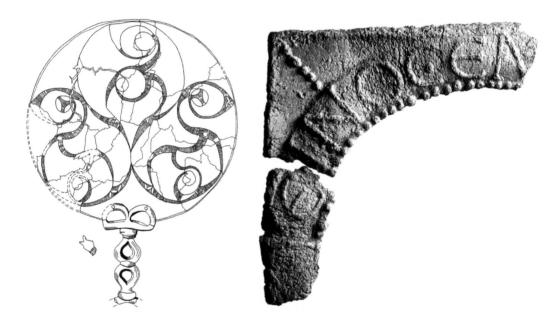

Above left: Mirror, Bromham, 255 mm long, reflecting surface 215 mm by 190 mm. (Drawing by Donna Watters)

Above right: Mirror frame with inscription, Podington, Beds. (BH-584656)

The little Petham *balsmarium,* or perfume jar, is a portable reminder of Roman bathing, a rare British example of an object known across the third-century empire. The visit to the baths, with its oiling, perfuming and scraping, as well as bathing, was a quasi-theatrical performance in its own right. It needed refined accoutrements such as this jar, with its frieze of cavorting figures around its body – a satyr and human with wine jars and two musicians, each figure separated from the next by a tree or a thyrsus, the staff held by followers of Bacchus. The Bacchic scene is common for these jars, its carefree keynote echoing the leisured life that owners would (aspire to) enjoy. Similar jars have been found in graves and the completeness of the Petham jar suggests that it too was once placed with the dead. For such a purpose its decoration was apt, since the procession evokes the blissful afterlife which worship of Bacchus might offer. Among other remnants of luxury bath gear is an enamelled swivel (Perlethorpe cum Budby), from which chains would have hung to suspend a flask filled with perfumed oil, and a panel from a chic hexagonal bottle of similar purpose, decorated with an enamelled plant scroll (Newton).

Balsamarium, Petham, 50 mm high.

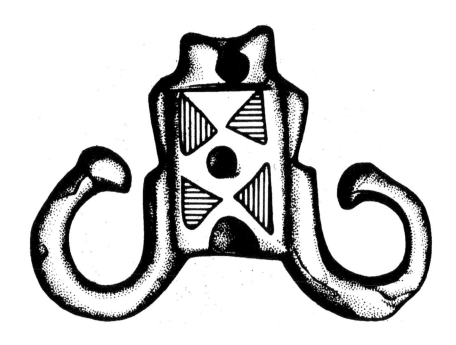

Oil flask swivel mount, Perlethorpe cum Budby, Notts. (DENO-54B3D1) (Drawing by David Willams)

Panel from a hexagonal oil flask, Newton, N. Yorks. (SWYOR-183D2D)

The Thames foreshore is among the artefactually richest settings documented through the PAS, reflecting the wealth of Londinium. Among the finds are numerous metal and bone hair pins which kept coiffures in place and served as hair ornaments. Most are quite simple, with spherical, conical or disc-like terminals, illustrated by a bone pin of mid- to late Roman date from Surrey Docks. Some have more complex decoration, illustrated by a later first-century pin, broken a third of the way down its shaft. This carries a female bust with an elaborate coiffure, exceptional both in its detail and in its self-referential character. Above her small face the head is shaped as a half-cylinder, cross-hatched to represent the many curls into which the towering mass of hair is separated. The points which rise at the top are the hairpins which fix the arrangement. Whether a wig or the woman's own hair, this would have required skilled preparation to put in place. The carving at the back may indicate some of the braiding required in support. The figure recalls the complex hairstyles favoured by Flavian and later empresses. These could be seen in coin portraits, exemplified by a silver denarius showing the deified Faustina, wife of Antoninus Pius (empress AD 138–141). Such images were copied by imperial subjects.

Above left: Hair pin, Thames foreshore, 71.4 mm long.

Above middle: Bone hair pin, Surrey Docks, Thames foreshore. (LON-F5778D)

Above right: Denarius showing deified Faustina, Blyborough, Lincs. (NLM-5533AE)

Chapter 7
On the Road

The dependence of Roman vehicles on Iron Age technology is shown by the names given them, *raeda*, *essedum* and so on, adopted from Celtic languages. Nonetheless, communications were transformed in the Roman period. These vehicles travelled on new roads, wide metalled routes replacing prehistoric trackways, complemented by bridges, causeways and harbours, all made to facilitate conquest. The many references to soldiers and supplies on the road in the tablets from the frontier fort at Vindolanda reveal the intensity of this military movement, as well as the problems of worn-out animals, broken axles and bad surfaces. Iron hipposandals (a form of horseshoe) give an occasional indirect glimpse of the animals whose labour moved commodities along the new roads. Much more common are the metal elements of horse harnesses, among the most elaborately decorated Iron Age and Roman objects. This horse-gear projected the status of travellers as well as keeping them in the saddle, complementing the rider's own appearance and bearing with the glitter and finesse of their mount.

The revolution in communications embraced more than better roads. Writing was adopted not only to commemorate the dead and pray to the gods but for more mundane purposes too. The transfer of information and coinage was crucial to the process of conquest, money keeping soldiers happy and supplies flowing. But cash and writing were not restricted to the army alone. Objects for writing show literacy in the rural population too, used to facilitate trade and maintain social networks. Monetisation, revealed by the hundreds of thousands of coins recorded on the PAS website, also facilitated participation in trade. Despite the improvements, travel and trade remained nonetheless a risky business and took place better under the auspices of the gods. Attempted mitigation of its risks may explain the numerous images of the god Mercury, patron of merchants and travellers, bulging money bag appropriately in hand for a statuette from Wickenby.

Metalled route of Stanegate, running through the frontier town of Coria (Corbridge), Northumberland. (Photograph by John Pearce)

Above: Hipposandal, Childrey, Oxon. (ASHM-1956FE)

Right: Mercury, god of travellers, Wickenby, Lincs. (LIN-3A2272)

The 100 or more linchpins recorded so far by the PAS, with dates spanning the late Iron Age and early Roman periods, comprise rare surviving elements of the chariots documented by Caesar as a shock tactic used by the Britons against him. The composite linchpins which kept wheels on their axles provide some of the best illustrations of the elaboration of chariot and other vehicle fittings. The linchpin from Adisham, Kent, dated to the last century BC or first century AD, is unusually complete, since the corroded iron shank survives, still connecting the pin's two decorated copper alloy terminals. The crescent-shaped head, cast in one piece, is plain on its face and rear, though its edge is milled with repeated lines. The socket to house the end of the shank has two raised mouldings with the same decoration. It is also perforated, perhaps to allow the threading through of a leather thong, connected to a small terret (metal loop), to secure the linchpin to the chariot's axle. The sub-triangular foot has a similar socket to accommodate the other end of the shank. The rear of the linchpin is flat and plain. Other linchpins carry more elaborate decoration, for example the curvilinear motifs on the 'vase-headed' type from Fressingfield or the bright red and yellow enamels on the pin from Hotham.

Linchpin, Adisham, 125 mm high.

Above: Enamelled linchpin terminal, Hotham, near Market Weighton, E. Yorks. (YORYM-B3FDA2)

Right: Linchpin, Fressingfield, Suffolk. (SF-1007C4)

The tigress found near Dereham in the Breckland is one of the most flamboyant vehicle fittings from Rome's north-west provinces. The animal's details are carefully depicted, either by close copying of a model or perhaps even from a sight of the real thing in a Mediterranean amphitheatre. On the fur-fringed head, for example, the open jaws reveal the canines. The back and right flank carry oblong recesses, once inlaid with silver and copper alloy to differentiate the animal's dorsal and lateral stripes from its body, though these stunning effects are lost to oxidisation. The body fur is rendered by longer sinuous lines and shorter incisions. The close parallels in a figurine from Banasa, Morocco, reveal how this object was used, namely as a fitting on a vehicle front, one of several felines arranged on either side of images of the god Bacchus and his entourage. The slot in the side of the tigress connected it to the vehicle body with a strut and the shanks, seen as stumps on the left front leg and rump, secured it in place.

Whether such fittings were intended to epitomise luxury, deter ill-fortune or lend god speed to travellers, the reality of wheeled transport in Roman Britain is likely to have been more prosaic, slow, weather-dependent, and needing constant repair. Nonetheless, carriages of the type represented by the tigress conspicuously exhibited the prestige of their occupants.

Above left: Tigress vehicle fitting from near Dereham, 156 mm long.

Above right: Eagle's head terminal for tying reins, West Ilsley, West Berks. (HAMP-E88954) (Drawing by Alan Cracknell)

Terrets were mounted on harness and on the poles and yokes of vehicles such as chariots to thread reins through and prevent their tangling. They show considerable continuity from the Iron Age into the Roman period. The Cholesbury terret is an unusual copper alloy example, quite worn, with its graceful hoop formed by two opposed horse heads. Between the ears is a circular perforation of unknown function. This hoop is attached to a broad moulding above the base or 'skirt' of the terret. Beneath this skirt iron corrosion product obscures what is left of the missing mount for attachment to the harness or to the pole which extended from the vehicle body to the yoke. The hoop's internal diameter (11 mm) suggests that this object is too small to have been used as a rein guide, but it probably functioned as a harness-fitting to secure a leather strap. The use of horse imagery on terrets is not common but nonetheless appropriate to function. More elaborate pieces like the Cholesbury terret would have stood out in form and/or function compared to more commonplace types, exemplified by a well-preserved terret from North Stoke.

Above left: Terret, Cholesbury, 47 mm long.

Above right: Terret, North Stoke, Bath and north-east Somerset. (GLO-8ACFA7)

Horse harness mounts are among the objects most frequently recorded by the PAS, after brooches. Despite its incomplete condition, an enamelled disc from Eccleshall effectively illustrates the colourful character of harness. On the back survives a stub of the stud which fixed the disc to a leather strap. The disc carries mesmerizing millefiori enamel decoration. Its central panel is inlaid with a chequerboard formed of mini-chequerboards in blue and white. Surrounding this are two further zones, the outer one white, set with an inner band of rosettes and an outer ring of delicate leaf motifs. The millefiori technique involves the twisting together and fusing of hot rods of coloured glass, cut into thin slices for inlay onto the surface of metal objects. Similar smaller mounts are, however, sometimes put to other uses, for example on sword belts. Their distinctive decoration, whether made in Britain or a continental glassworking centre such as Cologne, made them prized and widely travelled pieces. A cheek piece or toggle from Langstone near Newport (*c.* AD 50–150) illustrates the use of polychrome enamel elsewhere on harnesses.

Left: Mount, Eccleshall, 41 mm diameter.

Below: Cheek piece, Langstone, Newport. (PUBLIC-A435B8)

80

From the Roman frontier in the north, at Carlisle and Vindolanda, and in London in the south, come letters which moved along these new routes, using wood for their medium and written in ink or scratched with a stylus. Given the requirement for anaerobic preservation, such documents do not survive among plough-soil artefacts, but numerous objects attest indirectly to their making and circulation. The most striking is the spatula used to smooth wax on the surface of a wooden tablet, into which a message could be written. Some are plain, but more than thirty have been found with distinctive handles taking the shape of the goddess Minerva. On one from Hayton the goddess is recognisable from her high-crested Corinthian helmet, beneath which emerge her hair's stiff strands. The bust tapers to the waist, with a hint at the folds of her tunic, but no sign of the aegis, her distinctive cloak (see No. 8). From the waist the handle expands to an opening which once held the iron blade. Usually lost to corrosion, in one exceptional example from Highworth the blade too was preserved. Styli like the one from Piercebridge had a point for writing the text and a splayed end for smoothing the wax to correct an error.

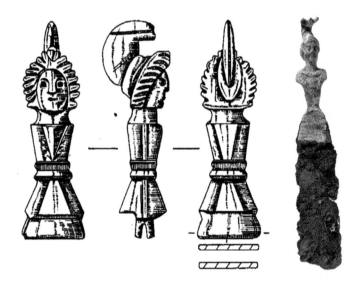

Above left: Wax spatula handle, Hayton, 75 mm long. (Drawing by Barbara McNee)

Above right: Wax spatula, Highworth, Swindon, 163.7 mm in length (the handle is 80 mm long). (WILT-9ECD01)

Iron stylus with inlaid mouldings and eraser, Piercebridge. (BH-D59607)

41. Seal box and denarius (NARC-B9DE37), AD 117 or later, Wood Burcote, Northamptonshire.

Seal boxes are small metal capsules of disputed function. They may have protected either the wax seal made after a document was completed, or the seal of a money bag (like that carried by the Wickenby Mercury). Of all the non-brooch objects documented by the PAS, they are among the most numerous, many hundreds being reported in varied shapes across eastern, central and southern England. The leaf-shaped copper alloy seal box from Wood Burcote exemplifies a type found across Rome's north-west provinces in the second century AD. Decoration with enamel inlay is also commonplace, though this specific pattern with millefiori chequerboards is exceptional. The holes in the base allow the passage through the seal box of the cord on which the wax seal would have set. On opening, this seal box was found to have been put to a different use since it contained a denarius of the emperor Trajan (AD 117), with a figure of Fortuna on the reverse, placed within, perhaps a votive offering. Some boxes, like those from Droxford or Kingsworthy, carry figural decoration. Eagle and phallus motifs are typical, the latter for luck, the former for speed as well as divine protection.

Above left: Seal box and denarius from Wood Burcote, 32 mm long.

Above middle: Seal box with eagle, Droxford, Hants. (HAMP-156A74)

Above right: Seal box with phallus, King's Worthy, Hants. (HAMP-069741)

A worn copper alloy arm-purse with four denarii was found near Tadcaster in 2005. The purse comprises two parts: a broad, bracelet-like hoop with smooth inner and ribbed outer faces and the leech-shaped purse proper, joined to the hoop by decorated panels, and missing much of its lid. Purses of this kind were mainly used by soldiers during the second and third centuries. The latest of the four coins date from the reign of Commodus (AD 192), though the best preserved is from the reign of his father, Marcus Aurelius (AD 162–163). Four denarii is a significant sum, a few days' wages for a legionary soldier of the later second century AD. This might represent the property of an anxious traveller, buried for safekeeping, despite the *Concordia* (harmony and stability) which Marcus Aurelius promised on the coin. Tadcaster, Roman Calcaria, named after the presence of limestone quarries, lay on the main route leading to York and the northern frontier garrisons. However, its discovery with the lamp (see No. 44) suggests the alternative possibility that the purse was buried as a gift dedicated to the gods.

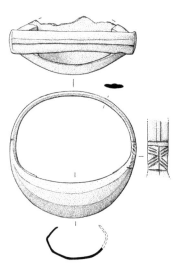

Arm-purse from Tadcaster (hoop external dimensions are 110 mm x 107 mm). (Drawing by David Williams)

Denarius of Marcus Aurelius (AD 162/163), with the emperor's bust on the obverse and Concordia on reverse, Tadcaster. (YORYM-5EFF04)

Chapter 8
Beautiful Homes – Deluxe Interiors

Home interiors are among the most difficult aspects of provincial Roman life to reconstruct, since houses documented through excavation are often reduced to little more than their foundations. Furniture rarely survives as more than fragments of stone or shale. Some inventories in the Vindolanda tablets hint at a world rich in 'soft furnishings', including hangings and drapes, which are never preserved. Funerary images too suggest affluent households, with tables carrying drinking gear, well-upholstered chairs and couches, jewellery boxes, pets and slaves. Surrounded by this property, the deceased gaze out from their monuments at the living, influencing reconstructed interiors like those at Arbeia, the fort at South Shields. Burials themselves also often contain accumulations of household goods deposited with the dead, as at Kelshall.

Above left: Grave goods from a wealthy early Roman burial, from Kelshall (Herts), including an iron lamp under excavation. (BH-84CCFA)

Above right: Vessel mount in form of satyr, companion of Bacchus, Gloucestershire. (GLO-E7D386)

The material wealth of the domestic sphere, what was used and stored in the home, also manifests itself in many diverse 'domestic' artefacts. Objects for guarding, storage, furnishing and lighting homes as well as for carrying out the routines of daily life within them, such as preparation and consumption of food and drink, are all attested among the finds reported to the PAS. Some were imported and others made in the province. In many cases they are richly decorated, testimony to the familiarity of provincial craftsmen and consumers with motifs from classical art and to the aspirations of (some) Romano-Britons to lead 'cultivated' and luxurious lifestyles. There are occasional hints at the realities behind this domestic comfort. The image of a sleeping African slave boy from Essex is a genre piece, copying Greek models, but it is a reminder of the exploitation of forced labour by wealthy Romano-Britons.

Above left: Reconstructed furniture from a wealthy military household, Arbeia, South Shields. (Photograph by John Pearce, by kind permission of Arbeia South Shields Roman Fort and Tyne & Wear Archives & Museums)

Above right: Figurine of slave boy, Essex–Hertfordshire border. (ESS-6F60D3)

The proliferation of keys and locks of many sizes speaks to the necessity of securing the house and the wealth contained within. On some very elaborate slide-keys the handle takes the form of a lion, an appropriately fierce doorway guardian. Of at least twelve examples recorded by PAS, the key from Southwark is one of the best preserved, the iron key itself being complete with four close-set teeth arranged on a straight ward. The recumbent lion adopts a 'relaxed' pose, paws turned forwards, mouth closed and tail flicked over its hindquarters. The stylised mane is a mass of furry clusters, the face flattened. Ring-and-dot stamps at the join of mane and body and on the haunches, and punched dots down the legs, reproduce fur in highly stylised form.

The copper alloy key handle from Fontygary, Rhoose, carries a double image: a youthful, cleanshaven Mercury on one side, identified by the wings emerging from the hair, and an older face of a long-bearded satyr or Pan on the other. This Janus image is well suited to a doorway protector but when viewed end-on, the features recompose themselves into the head of a boar, another ferocious threshold guardian.

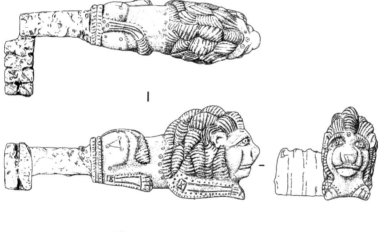

Key, Southwark, 134 mm. (Drawing by Chiz Harward, copyright Chiz Harward)

Key handle, Rhoose. (NMGW-C14CE7)

Most lighting would have been provided by torches and candles of wax or tallow but the Roman empire also offered an alternative, less smoky, light source in the form of lamps fuelled by olive oil. The copper alloy lamp from a probable hoard near Tadcaster (see No. 42) is a sophisticated example, its body finely modelled as the head of a maenad, or female follower of Bacchus. Her hair is richly detailed, with a braided lock tumbling onto on her forehead and waves swept back into tight curls. The nozzle beneath her chin has a hole for the wick. Above the ring-handle is a filling hole to admit the oil, and a large vine-leaf ornament. A similar lamp from London takes the form of Silenus, another follower of Bacchus, illuminating the aspirations of the owner to provide entertainment rivalling the god's parties.

Other illuminating novelties include candelabra and lanterns. The 75-mm-long tripod base for a candelabrum or lamp stand from Oxborough, Norfolk, takes the form of a stylised trunk with dolphins riding each leg. The domed lantern from south-west Suffolk, a likely Italian import (and donated to Ipswich Museum), would have allowed a greater control of illumination by sliding its horn surround to control the light which emerged.

Lamp, Tadcaster, 115 mm long.

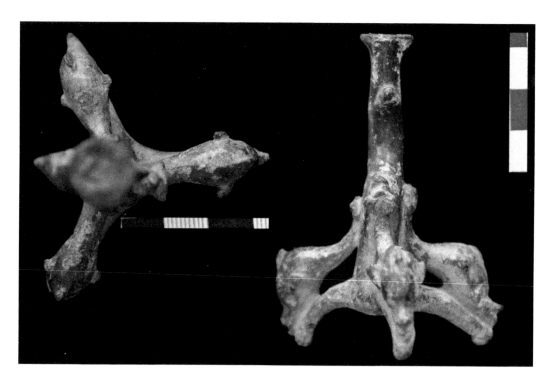

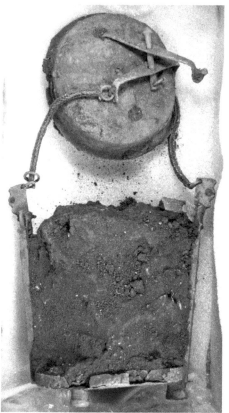

Above: Base for candelabrum, Oxborough, Norfolk. (NMS-E185A6)

Left: Lantern after excavation, south-west Suffolk. (SF-4BD264)

Furniture fittings from chests, boxes, cupboards, couches and so on are difficult to attribute to specific pieces. A second-century copper alloy bust of a naked youth from Capel St Mary is one such discovery. At the back is a cavity, holding the remains of a square, iron rivet that would have secured the mount to a box or piece of furniture. The face is round, the neck broad, the chest muscular and waves of luxuriant hair cluster at the ears and fall to the nape of the neck. The brows are finely arched and the nose straight. The figure is recognisable as Antinous, the emperor Hadrian's lover. This is not a one-off piece, since similar fittings are known from Britain, one from the villa at Littlecote, Wilts, and other provinces, which copy the emperor's favourite in this small medium. Images of youthful gods, such as Antinous, deified after his death by drowning in the Nile in AD 130, and above all of Bacchus and his followers (like the satyr on a similar fitting from Llangristiolus, Anglesey), were commonly used as motifs for such fittings, setting a tone of Olympian opulence and revelry.

Antinous bust, Capel St Mary, 50.8 mm wide across the shoulders.

Furniture mount with features of satyr, Llangristiolus, Anglesey. (WREX-C91A0B)

The purpose of some fittings can be more specifically identified, in particular mounts from folding tripods used as portable tables for dining or ritual. A mount from Pocklington is typical of metal-detected and excavated finds from Britain and the wider empire. Like the furniture fittings, it takes the form of an attractive male youth, perhaps Bacchus or Cupid, emerging from a calyx (stylised bud). The bust is nude though the torso is not modelled in any detail. The facial features are worn and the wavy hair is swept into a topknot above the head. The bust sits on a hollow rectangular base. From the back projects a square-sectioned shank which turns upwards at right angles, forming one of the hooks from which a metal vessel could be suspended from the tripod. From Darrington near Wakefield comes another tripod fitting, part of one foot; from the lion's head a stylised leg would have extended, with the paw placed on the ground to support the tripod. These tripods only survive complete when deposited with other dining gear, presenting the deceased as a generous host in death and perhaps providing for a sophisticated afterlife.

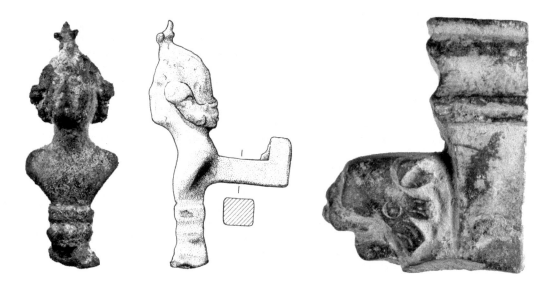

Above left: Tripod mount, Pocklington, 78 mm high.

Above right: Tripod foot, Darrington, W. Yorks. (SWYOR-1016E4)

47. Figurine of boy with goose (BERK-B60E47), Winterbourne, West Berkshire.

As well as mosaics and wall paintings, the houses of the wealthy were also decorated with sculpture. Some figurines documented by the PAS give us a flavour of this. So-called 'genre' pieces were made in the Hellenistic Greek world (late fourth to first century BC) and widely copied under Rome. A tiny bronze from Winterbourne is a rare survival of one such piece. It shows a chubby, naked winged boy seated with a large bird in his lap, perhaps a goose, which stretches its neck towards his face. With his right hand the boy holds the goose's neck, throttling or petting it! The original of this figure, the so-called 'Boy with Goose', is attributed to a Greek sculptor, Boethos, from Chalcedon in western Turkey. Its many Roman copies include larger examples in marble and smaller ones in silver, clay and bronze. The Winterbourne piece turns the child into Cupid by adding wings and the relationship between child and animal varies from the affectionate to the murderous. Another example of this figure was found in the Lexden tumulus, Colchester, one of several objects from this late first-century BC burial which were the likely gift of a Roman emperor to a British king. The style of the Winterbourne piece suggests that it was made in Britain.

The Caenby Corner miniature giant is also a figure with Greek ancestry. Snake-legged with a muscular torso and weapon in its left arm, it writhes in its death throes, cut down by Jupiter. Both pieces hint at the connoisseurship that elite Roman Britons wished to display to their peers. Other genre pieces such as the Hayton mouse did not need the same cultivation to be appreciated.

Goose strangler (?), Winterbourne, 56 mm high.

Giant figure,
Caenby
Corner, Lincs.
(DENO-075128)

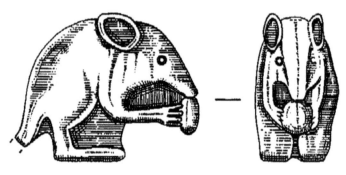

Mouse, Hayton.
(FASW-8B6455)
(Drawing by
Barbara McNee)

Of all the objects in domestic use, the best attested are metal vessels. In the last century before Roman rule their repertoire expanded from the cauldrons of Iron Age graves and hoards to include specialised objects imported from the Mediterranean and locally copied. These vessels served for cooking and serving food and drink, for washing in advance of worship or dinner and for bathing (see No. 34). More than 200 vessels and fragments have been documented by the PAS, among which the handle of an oenochoe (wine jug), found near two Roman villas at Appleby, is among the most stylish. Where it meets the vessel body, the handle splays as a feline paw. Along the handle is a raised rib forming the body of a lizard, legs stretched on either side. The lizard's head is at the highest point of the handle, beneath which the lion re-emerges with snarling mouth, silvered eyes and ears, splaying out along the rim as it dips towards the liquid. The metamorphosis between lizard and lion hints at the change in mood associated with alcohol consumption. Wine could be served in drinking cups; the helmet of a gladiator (*secutor*) can be identified as painted on a fragment of one such cup, a rare glass vessel, at Silloth.

Wine jug handle, Appleby,
127 mm high.

Painted glass cup, Silloth, Cumbria.
(LANCUM-91E341)

A hoard from Kingston Deverill comprises imported and local vessels. After discovery of a complete copper alloy handled pan during metal-detecting, the excavation of the deposit in 2005 revealed two further handled pans and two strainer bowls. One of the pans carries a maker's stamp, P. CIPI. POLIBI, i.e. 'from the workshop of Publius Cipius Polybius'. Made in the Bay of Naples during the reigns of Vespasian and his sons (AD 69–96), and often found at military garrisons, the pans served for heating liquids as lighter alternatives to ceramic vessels, though they could be used to as dippers for drawing water.

The strainer bowls were made in Britain in the decades before or around AD 43. Both were biconical, with the handle opposite the spout and metal feet. A strainer plate sat inside, perforated to let liquid, most likely alcoholic or medicinal, pass into lidded separate chambers, out of which it flowed through the animal-headed spout. This strainer served either to filter impurities or infuse the liquid as it passed through the chamber. One such vessel in a burial from Stanway, Essex, contained wormwood (the distinctive ingredient of absinthe), either to lend flavour or medicinal properties to a beverage. The find-spot near the temple known at Cold-Kitchen Hill, hints at these objects' burial as offerings to the gods after use in ritual, rather than as equipment left by the Roman army on the march.

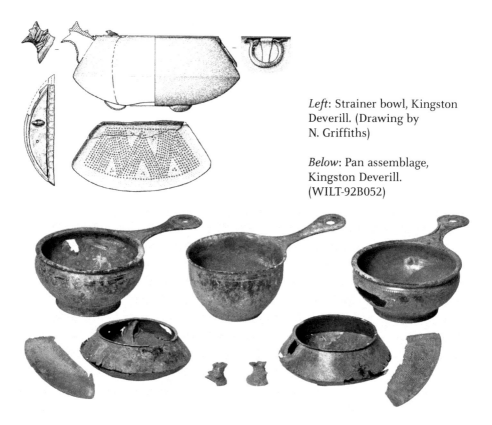

Left: Strainer bowl, Kingston Deverill. (Drawing by N. Griffiths)

Below: Pan assemblage, Kingston Deverill. (WILT-92B052)

So far, no late Roman precious metal hoards like the famous Mildenhall silver have been documented by the PAS. The next best thing to precious metal was pewter, produced in large quantities in Britain because of the ready availability of the raw materials for the alloy (lead, tin, copper, antimony). A large decorated pewter plate was found with two plainer examples near Bridport. Supported by a small footring, the plate has elaborate decoration at the centre, lightly incised around a low boss. An outer band is filled with a wave-like scroll, while within is a zone of oval motifs with their narrower ends towards the centre. This copies the fluting (shallow scooping) on contemporary high-status silver vessels found across the empire.

These plates must be a small part of a household's pewter stock – much larger groups have been found. Groups of pewter, bronze and precious metal vessels were deposited in large numbers in the late Roman period and their interpretation is controversial, perhaps votive deposits dedicated after ritual use or valuable metal resources (single plates of this size weigh several kilos) hidden in troubled times.

Whatever the explanation for its final hoarding, the biography of this plate and those like it embodies fundamental characteristics of life in Roman Britain. The province's mineral wealth did not only benefit distant rulers (see No. 2). In its transformation from metal ore to a presentation piece on a Dorset table, the Bridport plates remind us of the inequalities between those who made them, extracting the metal, casting and polishing the finished product, those who prepared and served whatever was offered on them (and cleaned them), and those who enjoyed their silver-like lustre as they tucked in. The raw materials may have been British, but in their form and decoration the plates, accoutrements to hospitality, linked diners to a continuum of taste and manners across a vast geographical space, whether they were conscious of it or not.

Pewter plate, near Bridport, 375 mm in diameter.

Further Reading and Online Resources

The full records for all of the objects discussed here, and thousands more, can be examined on the Portable Antiquities Scheme website (www.finds.org.uk). Typing the object's find number in the search box will take you directly to the record. Highlights from each year's discoveries have been published annually (since 2004) by the authors in the journal *Britannia*, published by Cambridge University Press. The following are suggested as further resources for Roman Britain.

Allason-Jones, L. ed. 2011. *Artefacts in Roman Britain. Their Purpose and Use* (Cambridge University Press).

de la Bédoyère. G. 2013. *Roman Britain: A New History* (2nd ed.) (Thames and Hudson).

Eckardt, H. E. 2014. *Objects and Identities: Roman Britain and the North-western Provinces* (Oxford University Press).

Higgins, C. 2013. *Under Another Sky* (Vintage).

Hobbs, R. and Jackson, R. 2010. *Roman Britain* (British Museum).

Jones, G. D. B. and Mattingly, D. 1990. *An Atlas of Roman Britain* (Blackwell, re-print 2002 by Oxbow).

Mattingly, D. 2006. *Imperial Possession: Britain in the Roman Empire: 54 BC – AD 409* (Allen Lane).

Millett, M., Revell, L. and Moore, A. (eds) 2016. *Oxford Handbook of Roman Britain* (Oxford University Press).

Moorhead, S. 2013. *A History of Roman Coinage in Britain* (Greenlight Publishing).

Ordnance Survey 2011. *Map of Roman Britain* (6th edition), (Ordnance Survey).

Salway, P. 2015. *Roman Britain: A Very Short Introduction* (2nd ed.) (Oxford University Press).

Tomlin, R. S. O. 2018. *Britannia Romana* (Oxbow).

Wilson, R. 2002. *Guide to Roman Britain* (4th ed.) (Constable).

Online Resources

Roman Britain: http://www.iadb.co.uk/romans/

British Museum highlights: https://artsandculture.google.com/partner/the-british-museum

British Museum - online catalogue: http://www.britishmuseum.org/research.aspx

Roman Inscriptions of Britain online: http://romaninscriptionsofbritain.org/

Vindolanda Tablets Online: http://vindolanda.csad.ox.ac.uk/

Historic England's introductions to 'heritage assets' include free downloadable overviews of Roman site types including shrines, forts, villas, and amphitheatres). Use the search box on the 'publication' page to find them: https://www.historicengland.org.uk/images-books/publications